Medieval Times

Written by Robynne Eagan

Teaching & Learning Company

1204 Buchanan St., P.O. Box 10
Carthage, IL 62321-0010

This book belongs to

_____

Foreword

Take students to the Medieval Times. This resource offers educators a host of enlightening hands-on activities that allow students to investigate this fascinating period in history.

Acknowledgements

Thanks to all of the students who inspired my interest in this exciting era, and Principal Vivian Bright for bringing Medieval Times to modern kids. The Laird of McNab would be delighted!

Cover photo copyright © 2002—www.arttoday.com

Copyright © 2002, Teaching & Learning Company

ISBN No. 1-57310-308-X

Printing No. 987654321

Teaching & Learning Company
1204 Buchanan St., P.O. Box 10
Carthage, IL 62321-0010

Table of Contents

A Decree to Educators or Parents,

Hear Ye! Hear Ye!
Venture to a fascinating period in history—a period when the seeds were planted for many of the beliefs, ideas and customs we live with to this day. With this resource in tow you can take your students on a journey into the heart of the Medieval Ages.

Medieval Times offers a host of enlightening activities designed to expose students to life in Western Europe between the years 476 AD and 1500 AD. Young learners will be enticed to explore ideas and beliefs, to identify features of the society, to describe roles of individuals and to recognize how medieval society shaped the world we live in today.

Through hands-on activities and active discussion children will experience the chaos, the joy and the pain of the times. They will see the role battles played in the changes that occurred. They will be exposed to an array of ideas and beliefs and science and superstition that were melding together. They will come to know villains and heroes, knights and queens. They will hear and create myths, legends and music. They will gain first-hand experience in leisure and work activities as they follow everyone from the king to a peasant child through their day-to-day activities.

Children will be called upon to use their senses, their knowledge, their skills and their talents to better understand a strange old world and the people who inhabited it. Don your cloak and pull up your hood as you prepare to unravel the secrets of a society that helped to shape the modern world we live in today.

Sincerely,

Robynne

Robynne Eagan

Welcome to Medieval Times

Copyright © 2002—www.arttoday.com

Welcome to Medieval Times in Western Europe—a turbulent period of conquest and change. Historians have divided the years between 476 AD and 1500 AD into Early, Middle and Late Medieval Times to help us better understand the character of the societies that existed during each era.

For hundreds of years Roman law, order and customs had ruled the tribes of Celts, Angles, Saxons, Vandals and Franks in the wild lands of Europe. In 476 AD, this Western Roman Empire fell to invading barbarians and the Middle Ages began, plunked between the Roman Empire that went before and the Renaissance Era that was yet to come.

Medieval Times, or the Middle Ages as the era is also called, didn't begin with a bang. In fact, some historians called the Early Middle Ages (500-1000) the Dark Ages. Law and order gave way to a chaos of warring and confusion that lasted for centuries. The years of struggle extinguished the light of education, advancement and compassion making this period a dark one in history.

By 1000 AD, the true Middle Ages were beginning. A stable society took root. People were cast into roles and depended upon to provide guidance, labor or protection to support the community. Settlements sprang up, a strong church emerged, schools of learning were established and order began to replace chaos.

By the Late Middle Ages (1300-1500) order and stability were crumbling again. A plague altered the power structure, a corrupt church invited change and explorers expanded horizons. Knowledge and circumstance gave rise to discontent and unrest that led to change. By 1400, modern countries were taking shape, common folk were gaining power and peace was spreading. The Middle Ages had paved the way to the Renaissance Era.

Artifact Museum

Historians are like detectives who follow a trail of clues left from the past to help them describe life and explain mysteries of eras gone by.

Think About It

What clues were left from Medieval times for historians to discover?

What to Do

1. Make a model of something you learn about during this unit.
2. Turn a 3" x 5" index card into an information card to identify and describe the artifact. Write on one side only. What does your item reveal about medieval society?
3. At the end of the unit, put the artifacts on display with information cards face-down.
4. The teacher will print a number on the back of each card. Classmates and visitors to your festival will record each number and their guesses regarding the identity and purpose of each item.

Medieval Western Europe Time Line 476-1500

500-1000 AD Early Middle Ages

457   Fall of the Western Roman Empire to the Vandals. A time of chaos and ever-changing territory boundaries. The monasteries preserved and controlled learning.

800   Charlemagne, "King of the Franks" crowned King of the Holy Roman Empire. Feudalism took hold. Knights became important in battles and society.

1000-1300 AD High Middle Ages

1066   William the Conqueror, Duke of Normandy, became King of England—a reign that lasted until 1087.
Feudal system gained strength.

1096-1291   Age of the Crusades.

1215   King John forced to sign the Magna Carta. The church became very powerful and wealthy.

1265   Simon de Montfort called the first Parliament, a meeting of the king, knights and barons.

1286   Alexander III of Scotland died and Edward I of England began attempts to take control of Scotland.

1300-1500 AD Late Middle Ages

1311-1315   The Great Famine hit Europe. Heavy rains, increased population and limited cultivated land caused many to starve or become ill.

1348   Black Death hit Europe killing almost one third of the population, causing a labor shortage and leading people to question their faith.

1381   English Peasants' Rebellion led by Wat Tyler challenges feudalism. Hundred Years' War between France and England came to an end. Landowners moved from farming to renting land or raising sheep. Exploration brought new ideas and knowledge.

1485   The Wars of the Roses ended and Henry Tudor became King Henry VII (1485-1509). During his reign, the Middle Ages came to a close and the Renaissance Era dawned.

Mapping Medieval Europe

By about 1000 AD the Germanic tribes of central Europe began to arrange themselves into the kingdoms that would become the nation-states of modern Europe. The present-day nations of France, England and Germany can all trace their beginnings back to kingdoms founded during this time.

Materials
large world map
atlases with modern and Middle Age maps

Get Started
Help the students find Europe on the world map. Invite them to identify the continent and distinguish current countries and their boundaries.

What to Do
1. Locate Europe in your atlas. Find Rome, Spain, England, Scotland, Wales, Ireland, Germany and France. Look at the surrounding bodies of water.
2. Look at a map of Medieval Europe. Can you find at least three differences between this map and the map of present-day Europe in your atlas? Write a list on the back of your map to summarize the differences you noticed.
3. Discuss the differences that you found with the class. How do you think these differences came to be? How have the boundaries changed over time?

Borders of the Medieval World

Copyright © Philip Baird www.anthroarcheart.org

Think About It

How would people have traveled between different countries and continents in medieval times? Why might that have been difficult to do? Aside from geographical barriers, what things create boundaries between people and nations?

What things can people share with one another once they cross one another's borders? Medieval Europe was isolated from the great civilizations that existed beyond its borders during this period. Vicious marauders, bandits, dangerous waterways and a belief that the world was flat kept Medieval Europe isolated. The passage leading east to what is now China was teeming with vicious robbers, as was the southern route to the African city of Timbuktu.

Vikings and Norsemen blocked the passage to the north Scandinavian countries, and the west was bounded by the Atlantic Ocean.

Fabulous Facts

It was not until the Late Middle Ages that Medieval Europeans explored beyond their borders to exchange goods, ideas and culture. With these exchanges came increased settlement, new ideas, advancements in agriculture, health and education.

8

Make a Medieval Textbook

Materials
8¹/₂" x 11" (21 x 28 cm) manila folder
heavy brown paper bags
three-hole punch
three 2" (5 cm) pieces of hemp, twine or supple leather
medieval notes, maps, pictures, etc.
scissors
craft glue and glue sticks

What to Do
1. Create a cover for this "ancient" text book by crumpling brown paper over and over and over again until it has the texture of heavy cloth.
2. Wrap the softened paper around the outside of the cover (folder). Fold the edges neatly inside and trim as needed to create a tidy look.
3. Remove the paper and paint the folder with paste. Quickly reposition the paper over the folder.
4. Glue the paper edges to the inside of the cover.
5. Plan your lettering for the cover text. Pencil it in and then go over the pencil lines.
6. Compile maps, notes, worksheets, drawings and pictures as you work through this unit. When you have a complete set of notes, you can place them inside the cover.
7. Use a sturdy three-hole punch to make holes in your cover.
8. Use a separate strand of twine for each set of holes. Thread it through and tie it on the outside of your book.

Try This
- Photocopy a piece of work from each child's notebook. Gather these works to make a classroom medieval textbook reference to be used in your class or in the library.
- Look up William the Conqueror's *Domesday Book* from 1086.

Fabulous Facts

*William the Conqueror sent representatives to every corner of the kingdom to find and record details about the property that was owned when he conquered the territory. The information was recorded in red and black ink in abbreviated Latin with Roman numerals. By 1086, a record of every place in England was recorded in what came to be called the **Domesday Book.***

It All Began in the Dark

During the Dark Ages (476 AD-1000 AD) the light of learning was dim. Monks and priests were about the only ones who could read and write. They protected and preserved written works of the Greeks and Romans and shared what they wanted to share. At this time books were written by hand by scribes using quill pens and ink to make intricate letters and decorative edging. Gold and silver were used to illuminate a page.

Think About It

How many books would there be if they took such a long time to make? How might the lack of books, flyers and newspapers affect the spread of information? How might this affect society of the time?

Try This

Write the "Fabulous Facts" that follows using only uppercase letters. Do not use punctuation or spaces between words. This is how the "Fabulous Facts" would have looked in medieval times—only it would have been written in Latin. No wonder few people could read during medieval times!

Fabulous Facts

King Charlemagne (800-814 AD) was a spark in a dark time. During his reign, he persuaded the scholar Alcuin to help spread education. Alcuin is credited with creating a standard style of writing that used upper- and lowercase letters, punctuation and spacing between words. We use this script to this day and can thank Charlemagne and Alcuin for making it so much easier for us to read!

Carolingian Script

The Carolingian script influenced handwriting and the letters used by early Italian typesetters—all of which affected our modern type. Use this script and a felt tip pen to add authenticity to your projects.

Freedom from Ignorance

Johannes Gutenberg, of Germany, invented the idea of using movable type to print books. The idea caught on throughout Europe and gave common people access to knowledge and information about the past and present, at home and beyond. With knowledge came power and commoners began to take their place in society.

The Pyramid of Power

By 1000 AD medieval society was organized according to the feudal system developed by the Franks. The system was brought to England by William the Conqueror as a means to control and govern society.

The feudal system was a social and political pyramid of power that determined how people lived. Those at the top were supposed to care for and protect people below them. Those below worked to provide the goods and services that sustained the community, but they had none of the power and privileges of their overlords. The degree of justice depended upon the character of the king at the top.

Materials
sheets of tagboard cut to shape a large pyramid when pieced together
photocopies of page 12
glue and glue sticks
drawing tools

Get Started
Talk about the feudal system and the various roles outlined in "Your Place in the System" on page 12. Draw a diagram on the board to help illustrate the concept of feudalism. Talk about what it might be like to be slotted in the various roles in this society. How would a person on the bottom relate to a person on the top?

Divide your class into groups. Assign each group a role within the feudal system. Provide each group with the photocopied description of their role, and the corresponding piece of tagboard. Tagboard sizes should correspond to the population size in the society, so they can be pieced together to form the Pyramid of Power.

What to Do
1. Paste the description of your role on tagboard. Have members of your group draw medieval characters who are representative of that particular role in society.
2. Get together with the other groups to piece together the pyramid of power.

Think About It
What system of government are we ruled by? Democracy? Monarchy? How is the feudal system different from the society that governs us today? In what ways is it the same?

Fabulous Facts

Henry II (1154-1189) made laws that abolished cruel trial practices of Ordeal by Fire, Water or Combat. He introduced Trial by Jury—in which 12 good men came to swear what they knew about the man who was accused.

Your Place in the System

 ow you lived in medieval times depended upon your position in the feudal system.

King

The king was supreme ruler of the kingdom. It was believed that he had a God-given right to rule the kingdom. Through conquest or family lines he came to own all the land and forests and creatures within them. He kept land for himself, granted some to the church and some along with titles, to nobles in exchange for their allegiance and services.

Nobles and Bishops

Lords *church*

Nobles, like barons and earls, held land and titles in exchange for allegiance sworn to the king. They supplied the king with soldiers, produce, crops, livestock and services needed by the king. They kept some of the land and shared the rest with those who did most of the work providing the goods and services for the community. Bishops were like the nobility of the church. They, too, had a great deal of power, wealth and influence.

Knights

Vassals

Barons granted land to knights in exchange for their allegiance and services. The knights protected the lives and property of the king's community and beyond.

Freemen

The largest group of the feudal population was the peasant class. Some were freemen and some were serfs. Laborers, merchants and tradesmen were free to move between manors and villages plying their trades or working as needed. They often ran businesses in the community or controlled small plots of land outside the castle walls. Payments or "taxes" were paid to the nobles in produce, goods or services according to an agreed upon arrangement or subject to the whims of the lord.

Serfs

Serfs, also called villeins, were like slaves, working sunup to sundown on the lord's land in turn for a plot of land to work and a hut for their family to live in. They had no power or freedom and were made to abide by many laws. Life could be extremely harsh for this group if they had a cruel lord. They were bound to the lord's land and could be bought and sold. Serfs could only become free if they were able to buy their freedom, if they married a free person or if they escaped and were not caught for a year and a day.

A Day in the Life . . .

Materials
4" x 36" (10 cm x 1 m) strip of paper per student (adding machine or cash register tapes work well)
drawing instruments

Get Started
Investigate the roles of the various individuals in medieval society using "Your Place in the System" (page 12) and "Medieval Folk" (pages 14-15). The kind of life you lived was dictated by your fixed role in society. What would it be like to grow up as a noble or peasant child?

What to Do
1. Choose a season, role and place and your age in the feudal society or select a known personality from that era. Think about what a day would be like in the life of your chosen character. Research to find as many details as you can.
2. Fold your paper strip into 11 equal segments. Use a ruler and marker to mark off time segments so you can create a strip diagram to portray a day in the life of your character.
3. Use the first space to identify your role. Write *A Day in the Life of* . . . in this segment.
4. Divide your character's day into 10 segments that identify his or her main activities throughout the day.
5. Display these one-day time lines around your classroom so everyone can put themselves in the shoes of the character you present.

A Day in the Life Challenge
Would you like to live in medieval times? Even if you lived at the castle things wouldn't be up to today's standards. Take the challenge! Give up electricity, running water, the refrigerator and gadgets and modes of transportation not available at the time. Sleep on "straw" and cover yourself with "furs." If you have a wood stove or fire pit, cook on it and warm water as needed. Keep notes. How did you feel? Would you like to live this way?

Create a Profile
Select a Medieval King, Queen, Prince or Princess and prepare a profile. Where did he or she reign? When? How old was this person? How did he or she affect the nation? How much influence did this person have? What did he or she look like? What kind of ruler or person do you think he or she was? Draw a picture to accompany your profile.

Become a Character
Use the information from pages 10-15 and research further to help you become a character from medieval times for a classroom presentation or your festival. What did your character do? How did he or she dress? How did that person speak? What kind of a person was he or she? Can your classmates recognize who you are?

Medieval Folk

The Ruler

A royal ruler had a lot of power, responsibility and problems. He met with advisors, oversaw knights and soldiers and was always ready to defend or attack. Many kings acquired skills and knowledge through their noble upbringing. A ruler had to watch his back as other nobles often felt they had a right to the throne.

The Queen

The queen, or lady of the castle, gave the day-to-day orders, raised her children and kept the castle running smoothly. She sometimes advised the king and when he was away she worked with the royal court to keep the kingdom together.

Ladies of the Court

Noble ladies led privileged lives with raised straw beds, soap, spices and fine clothes. Few medieval women received a formal education, although those of all classes were taught to run the household. Noblewomen often learned to sing and play music. They wore lavish and brightly colored flowing dresses and tall pointed hats with large veils.

TLC10308 Copyright © Teaching & Learning Company, Carthage, IL 62321-0010

Noblemen

In times of war, nobles led or fought in battles. In times of peace, they oversaw the kingdom and kept their battle skills honed. Noblemen sported some of the strangest fashions of all time—from long gowns with sleeves so wide they dragged on the dirt to short pleated topcoats with tight belts and padded chests, worn with decorative stockings and shoes with points so long they were sometimes strapped to the knees!

Children of the Court

Children grew up quickly in the Middle Ages. Some noble boys, but rarely girls, were taught to read and write by monks or tutors. Boys left home to train as pages while some girls left to learn dance, music and skills in household management in another manor. They dressed as adults of their class although girls wore their hair loose or in long braids.

Peasants

Peasant men farmed, raised animals or worked as laborers or servants. They wore rough tunics, belts, leggings and wooden clogs or shoes of thick cloth. Everyone wore hooded cloaks when needed. Women tended gardens, raised animals, brewed beer, baked and took care of their families. They knew the healing arts and did fine spinning and weaving. They wore long, dark dresses of coarse cloth. Children wore short tunics and were barefooted. Although peasant children didn't go to school, they learned practical skills. Boys learned to care for animals and tend crops while girls learned to care for a household. At the age of 14 a fortunate boy could become an apprentice to a master craftsmen where he would spend seven years learning a trade.

Outcasts and Wanderers

People were cast out of villages for breaking laws or for the fear of contamination. Those with leprosy carried a bell and called "unclean" to warn others of their condition. Huts were sometimes built and food was left beyond the town walls for these unfortunate souls. Escaped serfs and outcast criminals had to forage, beg or rob for the things they needed.

Folks Who Left Their Mark

Copyright © 2002—www.arttoday.com

King Charlemagne

Charlemagne was crowned King of the Franks in 800 AD, in what came to be called the Holy Roman Empire. This powerful king brought a sense of order and unity to Europe. He appreciated tribal customs; encouraged commerce; improved farming practices; revived culture and advocated for education, organized religion and just government. He valued education and new ideas. Charlemagne revived the Palace School at Aachen, persuading the great scholar Alcuin to design a curriculum. As an adult, Charlemagne learned to read Latin and Greek although he never mastered writing.

William the Conqueror

Some historians say the true Middle Ages began in 1066, with the Battle of Hastings when William the Conqueror landed in England to claim the throne he had been promised. William and the Normans defeated Harold and the Saxons and brought Norman settlement with French language, customs and a structured feudal system. To this day the English royal family can trace its roots to King William.

Robin Hood

Legends tell of a famous outlaw named Robin Hood, who lived in Sherwood Forest in Nottingham, England, with a band of followers. He robbed from rich nobles and gave to poor serfs, was loved by the commoners and hated by the sheriff. No one knows for sure whether this character existed or not, but some suspect he was Robert Fitzooth, the Earl of Huntingdon (1160 to 1247) or Robert of Locksley.

John Wycliffe

In 1380, John Wycliffe translated the New Testament into English and his followers, called Lollards, spread the word. The church opposed the idea of giving common folk the chance to read the text for themselves. For challenging the church and sharing the New Testament, Lollards were accused of heresy and put to death, but the text remained for all to see.

Joan of Arc

A 13-year-old, French peasant girl told French forces of the voices of saints telling her how to save France from the English. She was laughed at until her messages showed some insight. In 1429, she dressed in armor and led victorious battles that instilled a new mood of defiance in France. She was burned at the stake in 1431 by those who feared her, but the momentum she created led the English to be driven from France at the end of the Hundred Years' War.

Marco Polo

Marco Polo (1254-1324) was a medieval explorer who left Venice to travel across Asia for 24 years. He returned to share tales of his journeys. Although some people didn't believe his stories, others were inspired to expand their horizons.

Henry VII

In 1485, Henry Tudor became king. His reign brought harmony, peace, enhancement of the arts, compassion for the sick and poor and the end of the Middle Ages.

Trades Folk

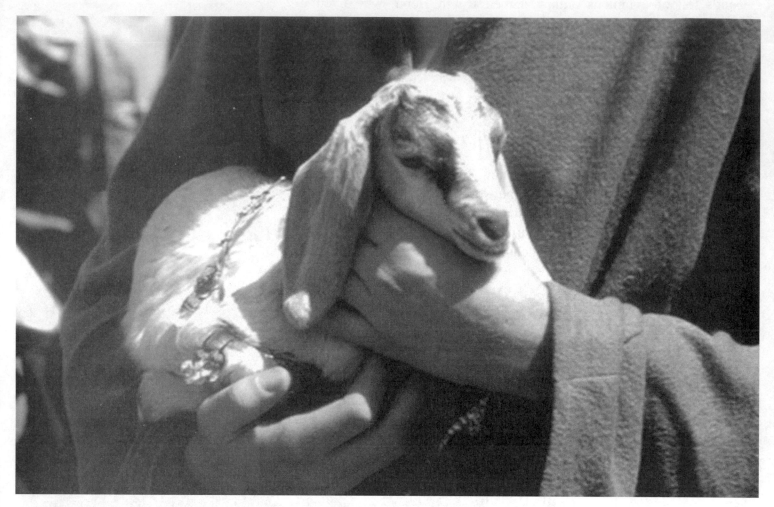

Skilled craftspeople traveled from town to town or lived in or above their workshops in the village. They hung out their signs and sold their wares from shops or street stalls in front of the shops. A strongbox or coffer kept their earnings and valuables safe at the foot of the bed.

A 14-year-old boy could become an apprentice and learn a trade for seven years before becoming a master of the trade. The apprentice usually lived in the master's shop, learned the trade and helped to sell the goods. Craftsmen joined gilds (guilds), gatherings of workers who shared the same trade. The guilds ensured that members kept some trade secrets, charged fair prices, used good materials and upheld the good name of that trade. The guild cared for members, their families and even the local village when necessary.

What's in Your Name?

Can you determine something about your ancestors by your family name? As the population increased, common names were everywhere—which made life confusing! People needed a way to distinguish between one Johnny and another. Identity was established by relation to others, i.e. John, Robert's son, by characteristics; i.e. Big John, or by the trade one plied. Henry V passed a law that forced Irish people to take a last name (a town, color or job) and by the 12th century, last names were commonly used.

Bailey: in charge of the inner castle courtyard

Barker: from the Norman word *barches*, meaning "shepherd"

Black: a specialist in dying cloth black

Carter: carried goods by cart and oxen, or made or fixed carts

Cooper:	made wooden barrels
Goldsmith:	worked with gold
Leach:	from the word *laece*; (leech) referring to a doctor
Thatcher:	made thatch for roofs

Hang Your Sign

A picture that represented a trade was hung as a tradesman's sign—a boot for a cobbler, a fish for a fishmonger, scissors and thread for a tailor, a sprig of holly for an inn, etc. Copies of such signs can be seen today. Why was print not used on these signs?

Materials
newsprint
flour or papier-mâché paste
water bucket
acrylic paint and brushes

What to Do
1. Design a sign to represent your trade.
2. Shape your sign using strips of newsprint and paste. Sculpt the paper into the desired shape. Allow heavy layers to dry before building over them.
3. Once dry, add color to your sign to help identify your trade. Hang these signs around your room, in a bulletin board display or at your Medieval Festival.

Rope Maker

Materials
dead cedar tree

What to Do
1. Find a dead cedar tree or some logs. Remove the outer bark and then peel long strips from the inner bark that clings to the wood.
2. Work these strips with your fingers to soften them.
3. Twist or braid pieces together as needed for the rope thickness you desire. To lengthen your rope, twist more strips onto the loose ends of the completed rope.

Weaver

Weavers used a variety of materials to make baskets, mats, blankets and fabrics. Floor mats and baskets were often made from rushes. Try your hand at weaving a place mat.

Materials
green and pliable reeds or bulrush	bucket
leaves or construction paper	scissors
strips	small block of wood
garden shears	craft knife

What to Do

1. Collect reeds from the water's edge with adult supervision. Cut reeds close to the ground using garden shears. Keep them in a bucket of water until needed.
2. With supervision, use a craft knife or paper cutter to cut 30 strips to $1/_2$" (1-2 cm) widths. Square off the ends so the reeds or paper strips are 20" (50 cm) in length.
3. Gently smooth each strip with your wood block.
4. Arrange 15 reeds horizontally on your work surface, leaving a space of about $1/_4$" (.5 cm) between each strip.
5. Begin at one end and weave 15 strips from top to bottom until you reach the other end. Leave about 1" (3 cm) of loose ends hanging along the edges for now.
6. For neat edges, draw a straight line around the edges of your mat and then cut carefully. Cross-stitch or paste the corners to keep it all together.
7. Turn the mat daily so the reeds will dry evenly.

Healer

Tribal people knew a lot about healing, but by 1000 nobles and church-men were having healers declared witches and burned at the stake. Healers often practiced their trade in secret and passed their knowledge through word of mouth. Medical science of the time had some strange ideas, so many turned to the hidden healers for cures. Modern investigations are finding value in the ancient healing arts. Recent research revealed that the use of bloodsucking leeches is an effective means to treat an infected wound!

Materials

string
clothespins
labels
mortar and pestle
vials, bottles or cloth bags

What to Do

1. Investigate the nutritional and healing properties of some common plants.
2. String a line along the top of a window. Hang the plants and attach labels to identify the plant's healing properties and health benefits.
3. Grind dried plants and store in the bottles or bags for display purposes.

Copyright © 2002—www.arttoday.com

Medieval folk believed in some interesting things like dragons and fairies. Their beliefs and wisdom were passed by word of mouth through generations. Knowledge was limited by the lack of books, education and communication systems.

The Universe

During the late Middle Ages, Nicolaus Copernicus realized that the Earth wasn't the center of the universe. His fear of contradicting popular belief made him keep his discoveries to himself until he was on his deathbed.

Materials

clay
pencil
ruler
tagboard

What to Do

1. Put yourself in the shoes of a medieval astronomer.
2. Look into the sky. Watch the sun rise and set. If you didn't know what you know today, what conclusions might you draw about the universe?
3. Create a model that could explain the movements of the sun, moon or stars.

The Magna Carta

On June 15, 1215, King John of England was forced by his nobles to sign the Magna Carta (the Great Charter). This document is considered the first bill of rights, serving as a model for democratic systems of government to come. For the first time the king's power was limited and even the common folk were guaranteed fair treatment. All sheriffs were ordered to read the charter aloud in public. Although King John signed the Magna Carta, things didn't change right away.

Fabulous Facts

The well-known phrase "The Law of the Land" was introduced in the Magna Carta.

Black Death 1347-1351

Between 1347 and 1351, the Black Death (Bubonic Plague) killed almost one third of the population of Europe and the Middle East. The death of 25 million people in Europe caused people to question their faith. It also brought about a labor shortage. An attempt to fix wages led to a peasants' revolt. Nobles were forced to pay for goods and services and for the first time, peasants gained a measure of freedom, wealth and power.

Fabulous Facts

Black Death was transmitted by fleas that lived on rats.

Expanding Horizons

By 1461 exploration and travel, the rise of a new social structure and political system, religious challenges and the spread of new ideas and knowledge brought the Medieval World to the brink of a new era. The Renaissance was taking root.

TLC10308 Copyright © Teaching & Learning Company, Carthage, IL 62321-0010

Traditions and Religion

Some Middle Age ideas were left in the past, some formed the basis for things we do or believe today and some are making a comeback. Tribal people developed knowledge, beliefs and customs that allowed them to survive, worship and celebrate life in harmony with the natural world that sustained them. People turned to Celtic priests or Druids for wisdom and direction. These tribal ways were considered uncivilized to the conquering Romans and their church tried to replace pagan customs and beliefs with Roman law and Christianity. Cathedrals rose on pagan holy sites, feast days were set on pagan festivals, symbols of early worship were transformed into Christian symbols.

Almost everyone in Western Europe came to belong to what today we call the Roman Catholic Church. The church was very important in peoples' lives. Some men and women belonged to special orders and lived in monasteries or nunneries. These institutions provided some education and assisted the poor and the sick. Nobles often left land and wealth to the church in exchange for prayers and forgiveness. The church, headed by the Pope and his bishops, became wealthy and powerful in politics, the arts and education.

Think About It
What important lessons could we learn today from the early tribal societies? Do you practice any medieval traditions?

Materials
research materials about celebrations
materials for recording information

What to Do
1. Make a list of some of the holidays, celebrations and spiritual events in your life. Record symbols and rituals associated with these events.
2. Find out how, when and where the symbol or ritual started. Did it begin during the Middle Ages? In Medieval Europe or someplace else?

Fabulous Facts

- *During the Late Middle Ages the festive pagan Yule and Twelfth Night celebrations merged with Christmas. Customs such as the burning of the yule log; bringing in of holly, ivy and other greens; and the giving of gifts became associated with Christ's birth.*
- *The pagan symbols of the rabbit and egg representing new life and growth of the crops and food sources became associated with Christian Easter celebrations.*
- *A popular wedding tradition began with medieval well-wishers throwing seeds at a happy couple to bring them the good fortune of having many children.*

The Castle

Between 1050 and 1450, hundreds of castles were built throughout Europe. These damp and drafty fortresses housed and protected the lord's family, soldiers and servants. Typical castles were built on sites that allowed the lord to watch over his lands and access routes. Communities grew within and beyond the castle walls to include living quarters, a church, market cross, priest's house, peasant and storage huts, agricultural fields and common grazing lands.

Most castles were surrounded by a wide ditch filled with water called a **moat.** A wooden **drawbridge** controlled access to the entrance passageway with its strong pointed iron gate or **portcullis.** From a **gatehouse** guards kept watch over the entrance and raised or lowered the drawbridge and portcullis as the situation called for. Towers at corners and along the castle walls added strength and provided vantage points for watchmen. Inside the thick stone walls was a large courtyard called the **outer bailey.** The walls were lined with **stables** and storage **huts.** During times of danger, livestock was brought to this area for safety. Within another set of walls was the **inner bailey**—a small courtyard containing the most protected part of the castle—**the keep.**

The **keep** was a safe tower with thick sturdy walls. The roof held the **battlements** and watchmen. One floor offered living quarters for servants and guests, another housed the lord and his family. In small castles, screens were used to create private sleeping quarters for the lord and his family. Another floor held the great **hall**—a long bare room with small windows and a roaring fire where the lord, his family, visitors and important members of the household took their meals and gathered. The floor was made of rough oak planks and covered with rushes. Interior walls were plastered, painted and hung with valuable tapestries. Large fireplaces brought warmth, cheer and smoke to the damp, dark rooms. Below these rooms was a floor for supplies and storage, guards or a kitchen. A **dungeon**, housing prisoners or supplies lay at the base of this or another tower.

Huts housing the brew house, pantry, dairy, goods and peasants were scattered throughout the manor yard and beyond the castle walls. The early **kitchen** was contained in a separate building but later became a part of the castle.

Fabulous Facts

The word **castle** *comes from the Roman word* **castrum** *meaning "a fortified building."*

Research a Castle

Castles dot the landscape to this day, reminding us of the power and influence of the nobles who ruled and the laborers who toiled with rocks of the domain. They serve as museums, guest hotels or homes to the descendants of those who had them built. Many are in ruins and some have disappeared. Prepare a short report on a castle from the Medieval Era. Consider Herstmonceux (Sussex, England), Edinburgh Castle (Edinburgh, Scotland), Krak des Chevaliers (Syria).

Two good resource books are: *Castle* by David Macaulay, published by Houghton-Mifflin, 1977 and *Castles* by C. Millet and D. Millet, published by Scholastic, 1993.

Design a Castle

Combine your knowledge of the medieval castle with science and technology, math, group interaction and art in a culminating project.

Get Started

Have students refer to "The Castle" (pages 24-25). Present a visual display of castles from around the world. Fill a bulletin board with photographs, calendar pages, posters, postcards and photocopies or printouts from internet castle sites. Provide a display of books about castles from around the world.

Discuss elements that were important in castle design, structure and function. Consider shelter, food, trade, defense, protection and power.

Organize students into groups. Expect each group to make and execute a plan to complete a model of a medieval castle. Convey the project requirements. Your castle must:

- be planned, constructed and presented as a group
- be no larger than 3' x 3' x 3' (1 m x 1 m x 1 m)
- include written descriptions of the various parts of the castle
- contain at least six of the following components: moat, high walls, towers, gatehouse, drawbridge, portcullis, church, stable, coat of arms, huts, people and animals

What to Do

Make a plan before you start. Use the Castle Construction Plan to help you get started. Make a rough map and think about measurements as you proceed.

Castle Construction Plan

1. Our castle will include these things: _____

2. We will make our castle out of: _____

3. _____ is responsible for making _____
       (name)

   _____.

4. _____ will bring these materials: _____
       (name)

   _____.

1. Choose materials: mural paper, clay, wood, paper, found objects, toys, commercial or homemade building materials, recycled materials.
2. Decide who will be responsible for what and who can supply the needed items.
3. Make a schedule. When should particular tasks be completed?

Try This

Combine medieval mapping with a little math. Find the area and perimeter of the courtyard, the keep and the entire castle. Create a corresponding scale so your model represents an actual castle. Present your castle to parents or students from the school community.

Fortify Your Castle

The Medieval Era was fraught with conflict and brutality. The countryside was divided again and again in battles over territory, power and pride. Many battles have long been forgotten but others changed the course of history and affected the world as we know it.

What to Do

Fortify your castle! Use the information below to help you add realistic defense and attack details to your castle construction project.

Hand-to-hand combat, surprise attacks, sieges with deadly attack weapons and impenetrable defenses were a part of medieval life. A nobleman's fenced gathering of buildings became a mighty fortress. Mounds were replaced by wooden and then stone walls. Arrow loops for shooting through and hoardings from which boiling substances could be poured were added. A moat was filled with water to prevent attackers from undermining their way into the castle. A drawbridge and portcullis controlled passage while curved stairs and other tricks baffled intruders. By the 14th century, castles could only be taken when inhabitants were starved out or tricked into opening a gate.

Defend and Attack

Copyright © 2002—www.arttoday.com

Materials

research materials   modeling clay
cardboard   string

What to Do

1. Make a model of one of the weapons listed.
2. Label your weapon and summarize its use and value.

Weaponry of Hand-to-Hand Combat

Most battles were fought by peasant foot soldiers who relied on strength, wit and simple weapons.

sword: heavy, double-edged steel cutting
lance: long wooden spear with a steel tip
mace: club with a spiked ball at one end
dagger: short-bladed, double-edged knife
battle-axe: long-handled axe

bludgeon: club with a spiked ball swinging from an attached chain
trebuchet: giant slingshot made of wood sent rocks hurling at a castle
longbow: tall, effective bow with 3' (1 m) long arrows that could pierce a man's armor from 90' (180 m) away.

Fabulous Facts

The cannonball and gunpowder invented in the 14th century changed battles forever. Knightly battles were replaced with a new kind of warring.

Try This

Many medieval inventions were connected to warring. Research and report on an invention from this era. How did the invention affect life in Medieval Europe and beyond? Consider the riding stirrup, suit of armor, battle machines and the printing press.

Medieval Battles

What to Do
Research and report on one or more of the following battles:

The Holy Crusades (1095-1291)
In 1095, Pope Urban II of France called for a war to free the Holy Lands from Muslim control. A huge army ventured thousands of miles across Europe in the first of a series of wars. Knights, monks, soldiers and common folk joined the brutal cause. Crusaders did not gain control of the Holy Lands, but they did return home with spices, silk and new ideas about medicine, machines and the world!

The Hundred Years' War
Between 1337 and 1453, England tried to take over territories held by France in a complex series of battles. The war ended when the English finally left France.

The War of the Roses

The Battle of Hastings

The Battle of Agincourt

The Peasants' Revolt

The Battle of Orleans

The Battle of Bannockburn

Medieval Battle Report

Battle Name: _____

Date Fought: _____

Who Was Involved: _____

Why They Fought: _____

Combat and Strategies: _____

The Outcome: _____

Make a Scene

Get Ready
Help students become a part of history. Explain how models will melt in and out of poses in an authentic setting to create a scene from history. Divide your class into groups of three to five. Have each group choose a scene or event such as an important battle, the signing of the Magna Carta, a feast or an everyday situation in a castle or peasant's hut. Use the school stage or a makeshift stage curtain for the presentations.

What to Do
1. Read "Knights of Yore" (page 30) or research a medieval scene, battle or event.
2. Plan how you will create a life-sized depiction of something related to this information.
3. Gather props and costumes from home or school to bring your scene alive.
4. Create a scene that can be unveiled as you melt in and out of tableau positions.

Knights of Yore

Copyright © 2002—www.arttoday.com

Warriors on horseback who swore oaths of loyalty to their lords were called knights. Knights were important in battles for land and power. Their deeds of bravery were rewarded with gifts of land and wealth. By 1200 aristocratic knights owned land, castles, titles and family crests.

Any man could be knighted for great deeds but most worked towards it from the age of seven, when a boy of noble birth was sent to another household to work as a page. The page waited on the lord and lady; did chores and learned about manners, religion, culture and riding and battle skills.

At about 14 years of age, a page became a squire, the devoted assistant to a knight or lord. A squire helped a knight prepare for battle or tournaments and fought bravely by his side. By the age of 21 a worthy squire was recommended for knighthood.

To prepare for the knighting ceremony, a knight had to become pure of body and spirit. He prayed through the night and bathed in the morning. He wore white for goodness and red to show he would die for his lord. In the morning he knelt for the knighting ceremony. He was tapped on the shoulders with a sword as the words *I dub thee knight* were pronounced. He was then given spurs and a sword as symbols of knighthood and from that moment on was bound by his oath.

What Does *Chivalry* Mean to You?

By 1100 a code of ideals called chivalry had developed. Orders of knights were founded on the principles of loyalty, courtesy, courage, truth and above all, honor. They swore to uphold the code and were expected to defend women, children, the weak and the poor.

The Classroom Oath

Materials
brown paper bag
India ink and "quills" calligraphy pens
pencil
fine-tipped markers

Get Started
Are the chivalric ideals of loyalty, courtesy, courage, truth and honor relevant today?

What to Do
1. Compose a rough draft of a classroom code of chivalry. When the code has been edited, prepare to make a copy to display.
2. Crumple brown paper until it becomes a smooth, soft, imitation parchment paper.
3. Use light pencil to print the oath on this "parchment." If you are satisfied with the look, use a "quill" and inkwell or calligraphy pen to cover the penciled copy.
4. When dry, illuminate your oath using gold and colored markers. Display your oath.
5. Have the king's herald read "The Classroom Oath" at your festival.

Fabulous Facts

The ideals of knighthood are still with us. This honor is inherited or bestowed by a monarch in recognition for outstanding service to one's country. Knighted men are called "sires," women are called "dames" and the wife of a knight is called a "lady."

Let the Games Begin!

Tournaments gave knights the opportunity to train for battle and demonstrate their skills. They traveled from afar to confirm their allegiance, share news and challenge opponents. Teams fought "mock" battles called tourneys or melees, and knights engaged in one-on-one challenges on foot or horseback. Games of the tournaments followed strict rules established by judges. A knight could gain glory and wealth or lose his armor, horse, honor or even his life to an opponent.

A Modern Joust

Jousting was a popular event in which two knights on horseback charged one another in attempts to unseat one another with their lances.

Materials
2 hobbyhorses
wrapping paper rolls
aluminum foil
length of rope

Get Started
Discuss medieval jousting. Use rope to mark the jousting field. Create a center line and two end lines about 15' (5 m) on either side of center.

What to Do
1. Turn your paper roll into a safe-lance using the aluminum foil.
2. Mount your trusty steed, holding it with one hand and your lance with the other.

3. On a signal, charge your opponent. As you pass one another try to break the opponent's sword. Touch the opponent's back line before charging again. Any contact with an opponent's hand will cause you to lose the match.
4. The first player to bend the sword of an opponent wins the joust.

The Game of French and English

This game, also known as Capture the Flag, resembles a medieval melee.

Get Started
Divide your group into two teams. Divide the area into two territories. Mark a prison at the far end of each territory. Provide each team with a flag to be hung near their prison.

Object of the Game
Members of one team attempt to capture the flag from the opposing territory without being captured and placed in the enemy prison. The first team to possess both flags wins.

Rules of the Game
Players tagged in enemy territory must go to prison. They can be released from prison when tagged by a teammate. Players can only be tagged when they are in enemy territory.

How to Play
Teams prepare a strategy in which some players guard the flag and prison, some chase and tag opponents, some invade enemy territory and attempt to take the flag and others tag and release imprisoned teammates.

Games of War and Strategy

Host a game competition using games of strategy, territory and takeover such as chess or Risk™. Chess features medieval characters and a theme of strategic takeover.

A Trip to the Village

Copyright © 2002—www.arttoday.com

The mist is lifting over the countryside as you reach the town gates. There is a chill in the air. You pull your cloak around you and adjust the trug on your arm. The cobbles feels cold through your worn leather shoes. You are glad mother chose you to go to market this week.

You pass through the thick walls of the village at the town gates. They opened at sunrise and will be locked again at sunset. You head for the market cross that rises above the heads of people on the street. It leads to the marketplace in the middle of town. The king's herald is spreading the news and orders for the day. Soon a preacher will take his place and spread the word. You hope that no sad case finds his or her way to the stock and pillory today.

You follow the dirty narrow street without looking at the gutter running down the center. You know it is filled with rubbish and filthy things. You try not to breath the stench—Mother says it could make you sick. A dog pushes towards the rubbish heap in the alley.

Freemen set up their wares on their front stoops. They live above their shops. Pots clang and voices call from the windows above. You wonder what it would be like to live in the strangely shaped houses of wood, thatch and stone that crowd the edges of the street. Some stretch out over the street. You watch out for wives who dump the family's waste and water into the gutter. You smell the smoke of their cooking fires and think that you would be afraid to live upstairs. There are so many fires in the town. The big house has a leather water bucket hanging by its door and a hook for pulling off burning thatch.

Apprentices call out to you. Do you need new shoes? A harness? A coat? Sledges pass and a cart with iron wheels trundles by. You know that a merchant paid a higher toll to enter the gates because his wheels will damage the cobbles. Water carriers distribute their loads and a baker's apprentice waves a loaf of fresh-baked bread to tempt you.

You stop outside the church to look at the windows. This is your favorite part of going to market. You know the story told on this window of the saint who killed the dragons. The rising sun shines through the glass splashing color over the floor. It is the most beautiful thing you have ever seen.

The elected mayor says "hello" as he surveys the town and discusses the new law with the alderman. You hear him say, "Everyone is unhappy about the rubbish in the street, but what can we do?" The smell of the bread fills your nose. If you get a good price for your cloth and can barter for flour, you might buy a loaf this morning.

Beyond the Castle Walls

The Peasant Hut

Peasant huts were simple structures with oak frames, walls of wattle and daub (sticks and mud), thatched roofs and dirt floors. There were one or two rooms and a central fire that provided light, warmth, heat for cooking and smoke. Beds and a spinning wheel were common furnishings and livestock sometimes shared one end of the abode. The hut was surrounded by a vegetable garden that fed the family.

Materials
clay
straw
twigs or craft sticks

Get Started
Provide students with information and visual examples of the huts.
Prepare stations with materials to accommodate several hut builders.

What to Do
1. Form the basic structure of your hut using the twig "oak beams" and lumps of clay.
2. Make walls using the twigs and clay.
3. Cover your roof with straw.
4. Add details to make the hut more realistic.

The Pilgrims' Journey

A pilgrimage was one way for medieval people to venture beyond their village. Israel, Jordan and Egypt were called "The Holy Land," a popular destination for pilgrims of the Muslim, Jewish and Christian faiths. Medieval folk tried to go on at least one pilgrimage in their life to a holy place to say prayers and receive special blessings. The faraway land of Jerusalem where Jesus lived and died was the ultimate destination. People from the same village or family usually set off together. For some it was a journey of prayer and repentance—for others a bit of a vacation!

Fabulous Facts

Geoffrey Chaucer (1343-1400) wrote a collection of stories narrated by pilgrims of varying character and social status in **The Canterbury Tales.**

Try This
Host a reading from *The Canterbury Tales*.* What does this reading reveal to you about medieval life? Chaucer used a London dialect that was common at that time—which differs from the dialects selected for print by the printer Caxton in 1476. It wasn't until the 1400s that English became the established written language of England, replacing Latin. Although Old English may be difficult to decipher, it led to the language we speak today!

*The story of Chanticleer would be appropriate for this age level. It has even been retold and illustrated in a picture book: *Chanticleer and the Fox*, by Geoffrey Chaucer, illustrated by Barbara Cooney, published by Harper Children's Books, 1982.

The Arts

Copyright © 2002—www.arttoday.com

Despite the muddle and chaos of medieval times the arts were not totally abandoned.

Medieval Music and Musicians

Music was a big part of medieval life. Many nobles were accomplished musicians who welcomed traveling troubadours who entertained at court and beyond.

What to Do

1. Put yourself in the place of a traveling troubadour of medieval times. Write a ballad about an event of the times.

2. Find a simple instrument and put your words to music. Sing it out!

Fabulous Facts

"Greensleeves" and "The Twelve Days of Christmas" came from the Middle Ages as does "Sumer is icumen in," (c. 1250) the only known piece dating from before the 15th century to be written for six distinct vocal parts.

Tapestry Tales

Medieval women spent a great deal of time with needles in hand—the peasants were trying to keep clothes on their backs while noble ladies embroidered works of art that told tales of the times. The Bayeux Tapestry, embroidered on a long strip of linen, depicts events of the Battle of Hastings.

What to Do
Use a length of linen or canvas and fabric paints to create your own tapestry tale depicting a medieval event.

Painting the People

Paintings from the Middle Ages show scenes and events but not the faces of the individuals. It wasn't until the Renaissance that nobles began to have their portraits painted.

What to Do
Paint a medieval scene that focuses on the larger picture, not the individuals within.

Spread the News, Spin a Yarn

Imagine a world without newspapers, books, televisions, telephones or e-mail and you will understand why the storyteller was so popular in medieval times. Storytellers told news of the kingdom and tales of legend and myth.

What to Do
1. Choose a legend, story or interesting item of news.
2. Write it so it can be told in about three minutes. Edit it. Add interesting vocabulary and details.
3. Memorize your tale. Tell it with gusto. Add some flair. Capture your audience with tempo, tone and volume of voice.

Art with a Purpose: The Coat of Arms

Copyright © 2002—www.arttoday.com

Warriors and soldiers always decorated the protective shields they used in war and tournaments. By the 12th century a standardized system of symbols, bright colors and metals was used to identify the family a knight or noble belonged to. The crest identified family traits and was passed from father to son. It was put on banners, seals and tombs as well as shields.

Materials
cardboard
scissors
craft glue
butcher's string
pencil
aluminum foil
acrylic paint and paintbrush
soft cloth

Get Started

Discuss heraldry and coats of arms using examples such as school crests, family coats of arms, state/provincial coats of arms and photographs of medieval examples. Help students investigate the various symbols, colors and language used on coats of arms. Refer to the list below for some basic symbols and their meanings.

What to Do

1. Design a simple coat of arms to represent yourself. Include symbols that depict your important traits as well as important events in your life, your country, state/province. Select colors that have meaning to you.
2. Cut the cardboard into a desired shape and transfer your final design to the shape.
3. Measure and cut string so that it can be laid over your pencil lines to create a raised pattern. Soak the sting in the glue and then lay it over the pattern again.
4. When the string has dried in place, paint a little glue over the cardboard and string and then gently cover the shield with aluminum foil. Rub the foil very gently over and over until it has taken the shape of your design. Let it sit overnight.
5. Paint a desired color on the foil. While the paint is still wet, carefully rub most of it off using the cloth. Do not move on to the next color until the previous color is dry.

Common Symbols and Marks

Badges could be divided into balanced halves, quarters or thirds using dividing lines. Various symbols represented different family traits.

crescent: victory over adversity
falcon: bravery
griffin: valor and vigilance
closed hand: strength
stag: purity and strength of spirit
tower: protection and defense
eagle: strength of mind
leopard: wisdom and agility
open hand: generosity
heart: loyalty and love
sun: splendor and royalty
dragon: strength

Fabulous Facts

Coats of arms allowed folks to identify visitors and hard-to-recognize knights in armor.

Gathering and Making Merry

Copyright © 2002—www.arttoday.com

Medieval life could be very difficult—with lots of work, lots of battles and lots of rules. Holy days (which came to be called holidays), feast days, tournaments and fairs were welcome reprieves to commoners and nobles alike.

Fairs

Large fairs arose in fields beyond the towns, bringing together local craftsmen, traders with goods from around the world, friars, nobles, commoners, beggars and thieves. One could watch a dancing bear or a juggler while purchasing wine from Italy and spices from the east.

*Include elements of a medieval fair at your festival (page 42).

Plays

Plays were popular in the Middle Ages. Traveling *Miracle Plays* helped to teach Bible stories to the masses. Members of tradesmen's guilds performed *Guild Plays* based on stories connected to the particular trade and often had a spiritual message as well.

*Find or have your class write a medieval play that can be performed for others.

Capture the Sounds of Medieval Merrymaking

What would you hear at a medieval tournament or fair? Medieval music, banners flapping, the thunder of hooves or excited whinnies, the call of trumpets, the roar of the crowd, a town crier announcing events, the clash of armor or merchants calling perhaps?

Banners blowing in the wind: shake a pillowcase.

Clash of armor: bang cookie trays together.

Cheers: enthusiastic friends cheering into cupped hands.

The clap gallop: With two hands, a pair of thighs and a little rhythm, you can re-create the sounds of a horse galloping across the green. If you are right-handed, let your right hand lead; if you are left-handed, your left will lead. Tap your leading hand at a pace three times faster than the following hand. Practice until you have the rhythm.

Fun and Games

Did you know that when you roll a marble, skate on ice, juggle balls, play with a doll or a toy soldier you are doing something that a child did in medieval times? Can you guess where Blind Man's Bluff, Here We Go 'Round the Mulberry Bush, Ring Around the Rosie and Hide and Seek came from?

In this era games were played by adults as well as kids. A violent version of football using a pig's bladder covered with leather was played. Nobles enjoyed gaming pastimes of hawking and the fox hunt. Contests of archery were also popular in every village.

*Host a Medieval Games Day, featuring games mentioned above.

A Medieval Festival

Copyright © 2002—www.arttoday.com

Host a Medieval Festival to showcase the knowledge and skills your students have acquired throughout this unit. Present projects, presentations, performances and a feast.

Medieval feasts required many servants to roast meat on a spit; boil meat in large cauldrons to become stew; bake the breads, pies and cakes over coals or later in ovens; and to wait on the feasters. The lord and his family dined at a separate table on a floor raised above everyone else. The royal table was covered with cloth and set with serving spoons, napkins, silver saltcellars and silver or pewter cups and jugs. Servants sat across the table from one another at planks, while nobility sat along one side of a U-shaped table that allowed servants to carry platters and serve. Thick slabs of bread called trenchers served as plates. Personal daggers were used as need-ed. French wine, ale, mead and cider were served to all. Throughout the feast minstrels played and sang and jesters entertained.

Materials
schedule

serfs to help set up, keep things running smoothly and clean up

tables, plank benches, "stalls," tents, period decorations

food, drink, dishes, serving spoons, napkins, etc.

medieval music (Celtic or Renaissance music is easier to find and will set the tone.)

games, performances, entertainment and displays (created throughout the unit of study)

straw or reeds to cover the floor

Get Started

1. Set the scene with decorations created throughout the unit (trades folk signs, models, coats of arms, tapestries, a castle entrance created with paper "stones" taped to the wall, heavy fabrics hung from the walls, etc.
2. Prepare a schedule and events list. Have a few dress rehearsals.
3. Create an invitation. Provide details in a medieval manner, using calligraphy, Old English, imitation parchment and scrolls. Provide details about your event and request assistance and items as needed. Find out who can supply what and who can help where through R.S.V.P.s. Invite families to offer their own medieval potluck dish or share a suggested medieval food, such as dried or fresh fruit, raw veggies, stews, bread slabs, salted meats or fish, Yorkshire pudding, cheese, scones, red or white grape juice or apple cider.

Come to Medieval Country

Invite students to create a guidebook for time travelers venturing back to the Middle Ages. What might they need to know? What should they take with them? What should they wear? How will they travel? What places should they visit? What events and sights should they be sure to see? What precautions might they take while on the journey? Include a festival map. Make copies available to guests at your festival.

Entertaining with Song and Story

Copyright © Philip Baird www.anthroarcheart.org

Traveling musicians and storytellers with news and tales were welcome visitors in medieval times. Stories and ballads were relayed with flourish to a spellbound audience.

Materials
Legend Cards (page 45)
simple musical instruments (optional)

Get Started
Discuss the traveling minstrels and storytellers of medieval times. Share some stories and listen to some ballads of that era. Think about forms of entertainment we rely on today.

What to Do
1. Prepare to write a story or ballad that you will share with others. Refer to a Legend Card or research a topic of your own.
2. Gather your information and write a ballad or story that will take about three minutes to share aloud. Edit and reshape your story so it will captivate your audience.
3. Memorize the tale and prepare your presentation. Add medieval flourish with musical accompaniment, fluctuation of volume and tone of voice, gestures, props and lighting.
4. Share your legend with classmates or visitors at the Medieval Festival.

Legend Card 1
The Legend of King Arthur

One of the most popular legends in the English language is the legend of King Arthur and the Knights of the Round Table. Tales of Arthur have been told throughout Europe since 500 AD. The legends tell of a young boy raised by an uncle who discovers his royal identity when he pulls the magic sword, Excalibur, from a stone. He becomes King of England and is advised throughout his life by a wise Druid named Merlin. King Arthur gathered the most honorable and brave knights from the lands to his kingdom of Camelot. The knights met at a round table that symbolized equality amongst the king and his knights. No one is sure whether King Arthur was a real person or not. Some believe the legends were inspired by a tribal chieftain who lived in England at the dawn of the Middle Ages and that he and his famous sword are buried at an ancient monastery in Glastonbury. Real or not, stories of King Arthur and the Knights of the Round Table inspired the ideals of chivalry that live on to this day.

Legend Card 2
Dragons

Medieval people seem to have believed in dragons although no one has discovered evidence to prove they existed. Many tales include reference to the deeds of these mysterious creatures. Dragons were believed to be enormous, flying, fire-breathing, creatures with scaly bodies. They were fierce and destructive, attacking and burning villages for food and plunder. They lurked in cave-like dens and often stole and hoarded treasure. Many tales recount the deeds of gallant knights or brave young squires who save people from the clutches of a dragon. St. George of England is renowned as the most famous of all dragon slayers. Could these stories be based on fact? Could a dragon be hiding away in a den to this very day?

Eat, Drink and Be Merry

Copyright © 2002—www.arttoday.com

A lord and his knights hunted and hawked for chickens, geese, swans and venison. The commoners raised pork, beef, mutton and caught fish. Most livestock was killed in the autumn and stored in barrels of salt water. Expensive spices such as ginger, cinnamon and saffron could make the salted meats more appetizing. Peasants survived on a diet of peas, beans, cabbage, eggs and sometimes a little bread and pork. Breads were popular but not available to most peasants and potatoes show up later in history. Wild fruit, berries, nuts and herbs were gathered and by the Late Middle Ages apples, pears, peaches and plums. Ale and wine were drunk by all.

Oat Cakes

Try your hand at this variation of an ancient recipe.

Materials
3 cups (375 ml) rolled oats
$^3/_4$ cup (95 ml) hot water
$1^1/_2$ cups (190 ml) shortening
large bowl
wooden spoon
(optional) honey or butter
3 cups (375 ml) flour
$^2/_3$ cup (85 ml) brown sugar
2 tsp. (10 ml) salt
1 tsp. (5 ml) baking soda
large cutting board
two blunt knives
rolling pin
cookie sheet
spatula

What to Do

1. Wash your hands.
2. Preheat oven to 350°F (180°C).
3. Measure and pour dry ingredients into the bowl. Mix well.
4. Add the shortening. Use knives to cut it into pea-sized pieces before working it with your fingers until everything blends together.
5. Add the water a little at a time. Continue to work the dough with your fingers. Keep adding the water until dough resembles playdough.
6. Spread some rolled oats on the board and put your ball of dough on the board.
7. Knead the dough and roll it out to a thickness of $^1/_8$" ($^1/_3$ cm) using a rolling pin.
8. Use the knife to cut the dough into squares about 2" x 2" (5 x 5 cm).
9. Use a spatula to move the squares onto the cookie sheet.
10. Put the tray in an oven for about 12 minutes.
11. Remove the oat cakes. Let them cool a little, then eat them as medieval folk would—plain or topped with fresh churned butter or honey.

Medieval Mutterings

Middle English was very different from what we speak today. Distinct dialects, slang and words from all over the world came together in a kind of medieval mumbo-jumbo. Some medieval words and expressions are still with us, some are in altered form and others have become extinct! Try your tongue at Medieval Speak.

hail. . . . . *hello!*
huzzah . . . . *hoorah!*
hither and yon . . . . *here and there*
jolly us now . . . . *cheer us up*
fare thee well . . . . *good-bye*
fine victuals . . . . *good food*
how farest thou? . . . . *how are you?*
tarry and feast . . . . *stay and eat*
prithee. . . . . *please*
pray hear me . . . . *listen to me*
attend the comely lass. . . . . *serve the pretty girl*
he had goods aplenty . . . . *he was wealthy*

Compare Then and Now

Record differences between a medieval community and your own below.

Compare	Pioneer Times	Present
housing		
food		
labor		
social structure		
government		
education		
health care		
religion		
transportation		
recreation		
beliefs		